S0-DSQ-141

WITHDRAWN FROM
CALARTS LIBRARY

BANNED POSTERS

EAM

BANNED POSTERS

presented and reviewed by **Maurice Rickards**

NC
1815
R5

EVELYN, ADAMS & MACKAY

© 1969 Maurice Rickards

First published 1969 by Evelyn, Adams & Mackay Ltd
9 Fitzroy Square, London, W1 SBN 238.78915.0
All rights reserved. Printed by Holders Press Ltd, London

CALIFORNIA INSTITUTE
OF THE ARTS LIBRARY

List of Illustrations

Banned Posters

The Poster has been under suspicion, more or less as a matter of principle, right from the start. Its engaging directness, its button-holing intrusiveness—and its often appalling bad taste—have engendered in the official mind a certain sustained reserve.

Even as an income-earning guest on the municipal tram-car, even (as in poster-taxing countries) as a source of Inland Revenue, even when called to the high task of raising recruits for Her Majesty's Armed Forces or of stamping out venereal disease, the poster has enjoyed a mixed reputation. Its early days have never been quite forgotten. Nor indeed have some of its recent ones.

Whatever its sins, large or small, late or early, there are none that shine more brightly—none so inescapably insistently—as intrusiveness. The poster has, to say the least, no manners.

Where other forms of expression have their allotted arenas, their screens and canvasses and proscenia, the poster has none. The poster has all the reticence and diffidence of the average theatre-queue entertainer; its function, frankly, is to intrude. However much the poster-advocate may tie himself in knots with special pleading, whatever nonsense may be written about Art for All and The Poor Man's Picture Gallery, there can really be no two ways about it : intrusion is what the poster really is *for*. It is not surprising that though it may often be thought to be pretty, it is also sometimes thought to be rude.

With a parentage that partakes equally of Bonnard and Barnum and Bailey, the poster has never been more than only just respectable. For all the espousal it has had from the arts and crafts enthusiast and for all the dignities thrust on it by the publishing of little poster books, the renting of galleries and the printing of reproductions, it remains by birth a guttersnipe. It is the Eliza Dolittle of the graphic arts.

It was objected to when it first came out, regardless of its content, almost instantly. The Society for Checking the Abuses of Public Advertising—born in 1893, and still not quite faded away—was one of the most strident voices of its age. It objected to the poster, as such, root and branch, paste and brush. Against the rising tide of what the billposters called 'mural advertising' it volleyed and thundered. It served as a rallying point for all who saw the dangers and desecrations yet to come. It had its victories, some of them enshrined in legislation that is still in force today. In its larger plan, for the total abolition of all outdoor advertising, it was less successful.

Like every other aspect of human affairs, the poster may be the subject of controversy on a surprisingly wide variety of grounds. In general it may be condemned as, by definition, intrusive. It may be condemned as over-numerous, destructive of amenity, ugly and unnecessary.

In particular it may be condemned as irreverent, indecent, frightening, seditious, controversial, libellous, treasonable, offensive, demoralising, untruthful, immoral, inflammatory, defamatory. It may also be an incitement to the commission of a criminal act, or likely to lead to a breach of the peace. The potential is enormous. With posters proliferating in their hundreds of thousands throughout the last 150 years, and with each specifically designed to be noticed, it may not be wondered at that some have proved more objectionable than others.

Sex, with its inevitable concomitants of Immorality, Indecency and Obscenity, has played a predictable part in the poster story. Jules Chéret, father of the French 'girlie' poster, if not of the French poster at large, was not the first poster artist to exploit the attention value of a pretty woman. But he was probably the first to make the point in a public interview. 'My aim', he said, 'is to produce, by simple means, pleasing, and at the same time striking effects. . . In France we have special dimensions for our posters. I prefer the largest size, since it permits me to introduce a life-size human figure. It

seems to me that no designs are so beautiful and effective as those which contain a human figure, nor, from an artistic point of view, can there be any doubt as to whether such a figure should be male or female. As the height of a well-made woman is about 150 centimetres, a poster 248 centimetres in length affords ample space for drawing the figure full length if need be'.

He went on to say, 'As far as possible I avoid repetition, and am always on the look-out for a new idea.' But this was an untruth. Among his many hundreds of posters, with subjects as widely ranged as ice-rinks and lamp oil, there were few that did not feature the statutory 150 centimetres.

His colleagues were not slow to adopt the recipe. Many, indeed, had got there before him. In their thousands, well-made women burgeoned from the billboards. Some were well-made enough to attract offical disapproval. Some became the subject of *causes célèbres,* blossoming almost overnight from a preposterous non-existence to censored immortality. Choubrac's tribute to Ilka de Mynn was a typical casualty. But she lasted on the hoardings just long enough to be remembered.

It was not in the field of simple indecency that the British poster made its big impact. The national talking-point was the theatrical horror poster. This, while it often carried its accustomed portion of female undress, was a penny-dreadful exercise in blood and thunder. In style and content it had reached a recognisable formula; it had become a national institution. It had also become a matter for concern.

The poster for *Rich and Poor of London* (page 11) is typical. In subject matter and treatment, as well as in the provision of a blank area for overprinting of performance details, it sums up the turn-of-the-century approach to entertainment publicity. (It also shows signs of adaptation from previous uses. The central dividing line, with its split-level floor and unexplained flounce of fabric, suggests a penny-pinching amalgamation of two separate posters.) For the scarcely-literate masses designs of this kind held a compulsive fascination. 'Unfortunately,' complained one

Folies-Bergère c. 1895 (France) *Alfred Choubrac*

writer to the press, 'there is still a large class whose tastes are so undeveloped that the veriest scrawl of a picture interests them more than anything written. The matter . . . disgusts every person whose morals are not already debased either by the misfortune of ignorance or by the folly, and worse, of feeding the mind on "dreadfuls".'

The 'dreadfuls' were a familiar item of the Victorian scene; it was by a logical osmosis that their influence spread to the hoardings. Often it was the publications themselves, directly advertised in competition with the theatre, whose blood and thunder brought complaint. 'Every sane and sober person,' said one sane and sober person, 'must have viewed with disfavour and disgust the state of our hoardings, which of late years have been given over so largely to the advertising of penny-dreadful serials. Murder and sudden death have been displayed in violent colours by certain periodicals and news-papers, whose only desire is to get circulation at all costs and at any price. We have grown strangely familiar with blood-stained knives, with green-eyed villainous-looking men, with all the pictorial embellishments, indeed, of the Old Bailey. That a serious protest had been made against these disgraceful posters, which cannot have failed to have had an evil influence on the minds of the ignorant and the uneducat-ed, proves that the nation is not quite dead to a sense of propriety and decency.'

The nation was not quite dead; it was as usual in two minds about the whole thing. As usual there was an impress-ive display of invention and resource in rebuttal. Said one poster advertiser, taken to task for his lack of taste, 'I admit the poster is a very thrilling one—it was in fact printed to produce a thrill—but it is at all events absolutely decent, which is more than can be said of the public advertisements of patent medicines and articles of the toilet, soaps, baths

Rich and Poor of London c. 1895 (Britain) *Anonymous*

only to become food for the moral destruction of youth. We do not think that the fashion-publisher should be allowed to escape condemnation. His easy compliance with the desires of those who have ladies' underwear to sell deserves the attention of all who wish to see the realm of advertisement kept clean. Advertising gains nothing from unclean association; it only loses in becoming a pander to bestiality. And in the case of the drapers with close-fitting garments to advertise there can be no specious pretence of the condonation of frank indecency by any spirit of high Art. The issue is a straight one, and every thinking person knows how it ought to be decided'.

It will be seen that the issue was by no means a straight one. At every level, moral attitudes were contorted. Sex, with all its multifarious shades and overtones, was more or less unmanageable.

If the portrayal of 'close-fitting female garments' aroused such excitement, it is not surprising that Canova's Living Porcelains (page 13) did so too. Presentations of this kind ('artistic, chaste, classic, unique') sailed close to the wind of the law. This poster, printed in Paris for a tour of Britain's porcelain-fanciers, was typical of a less easily definable category of poster embarrassment. It was destined, when the billposting industry finally stirred itself, to be banned.

In the uproar that was to break about the heads of the billposters it was the theatre-bill that finally blew the fuse. With ever-increasing daring, bigger and bolder posters battered the public. The touring companies, intent on ready-made full houses wherever they went, excelled themselves, Blood, thunder, sex and violence preceded them on hoardings all around the country.

Some of their posters were actually stock designs, over-printed with the name of the play and the company presenting it; the all-purpose illustration served merely as thematic bait. Often a small twist to the dialogue of a play was all that was needed to bring it into line with the poster. It was even

The White Slave Traffic 1902 (Britain) *Anonymous*
(The poster was banned on submission to the Censorship Committee of the British Poster Advertising Association in 1902; it was again submitted as 'Pleasures of a Gay City' in 1911, when it was again banned.)

15

(Three versions of the design show, right, the original poster, left, an interim paste-over and, below, the poster as finally re-issued. The poster was banned on the Berlin Underground Railway because of the nude figure; there were also objections by police authorities to the presence of the background figure. These were withdrawn after the figure had been draped.)

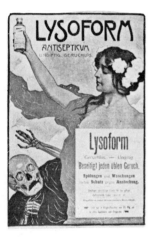

rumoured that, just as hack writers had been employed by magazines to write new stories round second-hand sets of illustrations, whole plays had evolved from stock theatrical posters 'sent up from London'.

In the tailor-made designs, in which the play was the starting point and the poster the addendum, details were permittedly more specific, shock-appeal often greater. Nudity—or *trompe-l'oeil* near-nudity—was a standard ingredient. Ankles, legs and bosoms abounded. It was the Chéret formula run riot.

Many of these 'large pictures', as they were often called, were admittedly gross exaggerations of the spectacles they pretended to represent. But the exaggeration itself was deemed an immorality. If the posters were not only indecent, but *misleading,* it was argued, they were doubly culpable. The public was being on the one hand demoralised, and on the other deceived. The critics had it both ways. The chorus of protest, muddled, unorganised and often at cross-purposes with itself, mounted in volume.

'Having a little leisure,' wrote a gentleman to a Nottingham paper, 'I was glad to take three of my daughters for a walk in the country. Passing by one of the hoardings, the attention of all four was attracted by a very large picture, representing, I suppose, a scene in a play then running at one of the theatres. A more senseless, idotic scene could not well be imagined. The picture was not only lacking in good taste, and in every element that could give pleasure to those that looked at it, but representing women whose rude nakedness cannot be said to have been covered; it was in my judgement positively indecent.

'I dropped my eyes with shame; my children did the same, and we passed on without a word. This week we are treated to another large picture on the walls—again a representation of a scene in a theatre.

'Here we have what appears to be a Bacchanalian orgy, brought, in theatrical phrase, "up-to-date"—a monstrous thing; and, of course, among the rest we had a full allowance of scantily-dressed women.

'I do not know that these pictures are exceptional. I mention them because they are the most recent. I am not now proposing to discuss the propriety of such plays as these pictures illustrate being played in the theatre itself ... I am only asking now whether theatre managers are justified in thrusting before the eyes of everybody these representations ... That there is no law to restrain them from doing so I infer from the fact that we have a succession of such pictures all through the year, and the authorities do not interfere. I do not ask, are the managers acting within their legal rights? but are they acting fairly and honourably towards the public at large? I say they are not.'

It may be wondered how he would have reacted to the continental scene. It was at about this time that Willette's poster for *La Revue Déshabillée* (page 21) was running into censorship trouble in Paris. Here the complaint was not so much the nudity of the girl but the presence of the male silhouette looming over her. By comparison with British standards the French censorship (which was centralised) was easy-going. British censorship, though uncoordinated, and vested largely in the readers' correspondence columns of the press, was relatively rigid.

In Germany it was often more so. When the printed poster for the Bavarian National Exhibition was shown to the publicity committee there was consternation at the nakedness of the artisan-children (page 23). After long discussion and weighing of costs of a reprint it was decided to scrap the whole run. The artist was asked to amend the original drawing to provide discreet concealment.

In Britain the rising tide of protest and prosecution could no longer be ignored. The billposters decided to grasp the nettle; they would take action themselves, before anyone else did. 'In the past,' said *The Bill Poster,* 'the advertiser's own interest has been thought to be sufficient safe-guard against posters of an objectionable nature being put out, but the experience of the last few years . . . proves that unless the trade itself exercises a strict supervision, the control will pass into other hands; this we ought to do since it will be done by others; the more faults we correct, the fewer we shall leave to our reproach.' The threat of an official censorship *à la francaise* had become real.

It must be recalled that the billposting industry, which was responsible neither for the design nor the production of the posters it dealt with, existed merely to offer them display space. Emerging from the near-anarchy of their founding fathers, the 'bill-stickers' had long since turned respectable. Gone were the fly-by-nights who plastered bills up indiscriminately—often one on top of the other in competitive profusion. Gone also were the strong-arm lookout men, employed to ward off rival operators. Instead there was a more or less disciplined industry—billposting companies with their own specially appointed sites, contracts with leading advertisers, respectable addresses with headed notepaper and even in some cases telephone numbers. There were also two Trade Associations.

The billposters saw that their new respectability was at risk. The two associations, the London Billposters Protection Association and the United Billposters Association, joined forces in 1890 to form the world's first voluntary censorship committee. The idea was simple. They would themselves vet the posters that their customers asked them to put up.

It was an idea that was to be adopted in other fields, notably, and for similar reasons, by the film industry, a quarter of a century later. Self-regulation was recognised not only as socially desirable—but as cheaper. With doubtful material filtered out at the source, the risk of costly legal actions—not to mention costly withdrawals and modifications—was thereby reduced to a minimum.

For the billposters it was a pioneering act of cooperation. Each agreed to abide by the decision of the jointly-appointed

La Revue Déshabillée c. 1896 (France) *Adolphe Willette*

LA REVUE DÉSHABILLÉE

de

M. Jean d'Arc

A. Willette

Tous les Soirs

Au Concert des Ambassadeurs

Censorship Committee. Any member receiving a poster that caused him concern was to submit it to the Committee. If the Committee turned it down, no member would display it. All were indemnified against action for breach of contract. To their clients, the advertisers, the industry presented a united front. The idea worked. In the whole history of cooperative action there have been few examples as consistently successful. (Today, some 80 years on, the idea still works.)

Perhaps the true heroine of the Poster Nineties—and perhaps the true progenitor of the Censorship Committee of the United Billposters Association—was Zaeo.

If the average Londoner found her name unpronounceable, there was little enough confusion about the rest of her. She was, quite literally, the central figure in a row that nearly closed the Royal Aquarium—and brought it romping back to success and solvency. Her ultimate suppression proved so effective that no visual trace of her survives. Her story is without a picture.

The Royal Aquarium, an entertainment centre that had never quite caught on, was a dark Victorian building that stood where the Central Hall, Westminster, now stands. Uncertain of its true role in life—its very title an anomaly, for the fish had disappeared shortly after it had opened—it took to the mounting of General Attractions. These, like those of the Royal Agricultural Hall and Olympia, included exhibitions, circuses, dramatic presentations, acrobatic performances and anything else that the management could think of. In a commanding position just across the road from Westminster Abbey and the Houses of Parliament, the building attracted, if not much in the way of turnstile customers, a lot of attention.

One of the things the management thought of was Zaeo. As the star of an acrobatic troupe, her performance was no more extraordinary than those of many other performers. She was a

Bavarian National Exhibition 1896 (Germany) *Riemerschmid*
(Above, before amendment; below, after)

HARRY NORRIS & HERBERT CLAYTON'S FARCICAL COMEDY REVUE

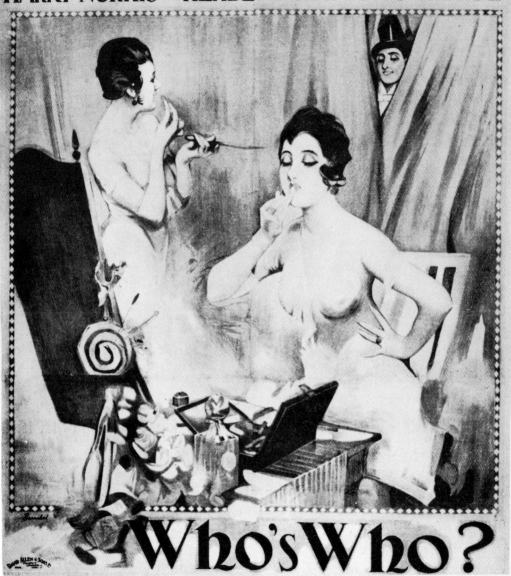

Who's Who?

competent acrobat. What distinguished her from the others was her picture on the placards in front of the house.

In this rendering, according to Mr Coote of the National Vigilance Society, Zaeo was indecent. With her flesh-pink tights, her fulsome figure, her low-cut neck and her allegedly acrobatic posture she as an affront to all right-thinking people. Londoners had become accustomed, he said, to advertisements of all kinds of brutality, yet up to the time when Zaeo picture was flaunted before the eyes of the public, there had been 'no previous parallel for the offensiveness, grossness, vulgarity and indecency of hoarding pictures'.

It is tantalising that no copy of Zaeo has survived; we can only guess at the validity of Mr Coote's objection. But it is clear the Mr Coote was gravely disturbed. 'So dexterously has the picture been drawn,' he said, eyeing it narrowly, 'that as men of the world, Londoners must be led to the conviction that this lady actually appeared in the same nude condition.'

From Mr Coote's description it would seem that Zaeo's low-cut neck and fulsome figure were but the shape of things to come. Bosoms have loomed large in poster history. Twenty years later, in another bosom scandal, the *Who's Who* poster was to run into similar trouble. In the illustration here a 1916 Zaeo appears in her pre-censorship ensemble. (Her respectable one appears on page 48.) She is here perhaps as close as we will ever get to the original Zaeo.

Mr Coote was speaking at a hearing of the Theatre and Music Hall Committee of the London County Council at which the management of the Royal Aquarium had applied for a renewal of its licence. Mr Coote opposed the renewal. Mr Coote had behind him the full weight not only of the National Vigilance Society but also of a number of right-minded and distinguished people who, unfortunately, 'owing to the opprobrium and catcalls that were normally the lot of objectors in cases of this sort,' preferred not to have their names mentioned.

In passing it would be interesting to compare the apparent

Who's Who? 1916 (Britain) *W. H. Barribal*
(The amended version appears on page 48)

DALY'S THEATRE

Sole Lessee and Manager,
Mr AUGUSTIN DALY.

AN ARTIST'S MODEL

GEORGE EDWARDES' COMPANY

Julius Price

WATERLOW & SONS LD
LITH WALL
LONDON LONDON
COPYRIGHT E.C.

undress of Zaeo with the straightforward nudity, only a few years later, of Julius Price's *An Artist's Model* and Félicien Rops' confection (page 29) for his own one-man show. Both of these fell foul of their respective censors, but the artist's model was eventually allowed out with a much-enlarged palette, and the Rops lady, whose palette had never had more than the smallest pretensions to adequacy, was finally allowed out just as she was. In Austria, Klimt's poster for the *Secession* art exhibition (page 31) got by with the addition of a bit of stylised forestry.

Mr Coote's indictment of Zaeo was thunderous and comprehensive. It occupied more than half a morning. After a conscientious hearing the London County Council concurred.

They made the renewal of the Aquarium's licence conditional (as usual) on the exclusion of prostitutes and, on this occasion, on the removal of the posters. There was also a prohibition on the sale of pamphlets, postcards and any other printed matter showing the pictures (The Aquarium had reputedly sold some hundreds of thousands of postcard reproductions of the poster. These too appear to have vanished without trace.)

The London County Council ruling was a spectacular victory for the National Vigilance Society. But it must not be supposed that it was a universally popular one. The case roused comment in papers as widely varied as the *New York Times* and the London *Bakers' Record.* Among the many who took leave to question the decision was the *Financial Times,* although its commentator was quick to see the silver lining: 'Zaeo . . . may be credited with a goodly portion of the improvement in the Aquarium treasury, and, without wishing for a moment to detract from the attractive powers of the young lady herself, we must express the opinion that her success as a "draw" is largely due to the way in which she has been "warmed up" to stimulate the public taste. The Aquarium had the good luck to hit upon a design for advertising Zaeo's presence which caught the eagle—not to say evil—eyes of the narrow-minded busybodies who are the

An Artist's Model c. 1910 (Britain) *Julius Price*

27

modern male personifications of that almost defunct essence of decency—the British Matron.

'Because the artiste was portrayed as going through her gymnastic feats in a suitable costume, which, needless to say, does not include a dress with a six-foot train, these Pecksniffs of the streets raised a prurient howl that has effectually put the Aquarium on its feet again . . . No less than £12,790 7s. 8d. has been taken at the doors for admissions to 30th June, without reckoning season tickets and reserved seats . . . Much of this has been contributed by persons who, for various motives, have been to see the original of the famous poster. Some because they wanted to see if Zaeo's dress was really naughty, some because they hoped it was, that they might howl with the howlers, and some because they hoped it was as bad as it was said to be so that they might gloat over the alleged naughtiness for its own sake.

'Needless to say, many of these people have been disappointed—except such as went to see a bona fide gymnastic performance, for there is nothing in Zaeo's dress to which anyone, short of those who put trousers on the legs of their pianos, need object. But this curiosity has had the desired effect of putting the Aquarium shareholders on good terms with themselves.

'We congratulate them on the way in which an attack upon their rights has been adroitly turned to their advantage, for if vested interest were to be at the mercy of half-witted tub-thumpers, may reputable and profitable sources of income would be closed'.

It will be seen that, on more than purely moral grounds, opinion was divided. Other papers, ever ready to distract the argument from its central focus, attacked inconsistencies. Said one leading article, 'the people who excite themselves on the subject of the Zaeo advertisement should devote their efforts to amending the style of undress affected by the feminine portion of the *audience* at theatres, which really calls

Exposition Rops 1896 (France) *Félicien Rops*

28

for animadversion more than a mere poster on a wall. Granting that the latter be somewhat realistic the former is absolute reality. In the one case there is need to hunt about for or imagine some suggestive characteristic in order to condemn it; indecency and vulgarity are pretty plainly exposed to public view by most women who sit at London theatres.'

In similar vein, the man who might have been supposed to know the most about it, Zaeo's father himself : 'I consider for a gymnast's dress Zaeo's is modestly designed. My other daughter, Zazel, performed in the Royal Aquarium for two years, also in Edinburgh and the principal cities in England, in the same dress as now worn by Zaeo, and I never heard a word against it—although it was then cut much lower at the breast, similar,' (Mr Zaeo could not resist the point) 'similar to dresses worn at Her Majesty's drawing room.'

It must be said that those who defended the freedom of the hoardings betrayed a partisanship as blinkered as that of their assailants. Logical or otherwise, the expression of opinion on either side was rarely moderate; often the arguments were as specious as they were assertive. One commentator declared that the rise in crimes of violence was directly attributable to the hoardings. Another as confidently hailed hoardings as the poor man's picture gallery: 'I believe they have an educating and refining influence over a certain class . . . many people without a knowledge of letters have gradually learnt their ABC from the few words of letterpress attached to wall pictures. This is especially the case in the country villages, for posters are now everywhere, and in Wales, people born before School Board days have gradually picked up enough English to enable them to understand an English newspaper.'

It was perhaps in a spirit of exhausted compromise that the suggestion was again revived for the taxing of advertisements. This idea was seen by the billposters as a serious threat; who could tell what havoc a tax might play in the economy of the

Secession Art Exhibition c. 1910 (Austria) *Gustav Klimt* (Above, before amendment; below, after)

billboards? For years, the idea had been the billposters' nightmare.

The call became more insistent. If the offensive posters could not be got rid of without all this fuss, why not tax them out of existence? At least, this way, they could be turned to the public advantage. On the continent, where posters were taxed, they did not have these troubles. And even if in the British case a tax were found not to do away with them altogether, at least 'we could still gaze on the various indecent, hideous or ludicrous illustrations with the comforting reflection that they represented not only the dubious wares of the enterprising showman or tradesman, but also so much good money in the public purse.' However doubtful the ethics of the argument, the idea was attractive. Eyes turned to the Continent.

But the situation on the continent was less simple than it seemed. Some countries taxed; some did not. Some had stringent censorship; others had not. Not only from country to country, but from province to province, practise varied. In some places the censor had become a recognised Aunt Sally.

Typical of the running dialogue that was sometimes allowed to develop between poster men and local censorship was the poster put out by a Berlin printing firm. 'The Chief of Police,' it said, 'has no objection to *good* posters'. The statement, appearing not long after a police clamp-down on an earlier poster, was thought by its publishers to be beyond reproach. As a statement of fact it was unassailable.

The Polizeipräsident, not to be mocked even slightly, disallowed it. Continued publication was permitted only after a blank sticker had converted the Polizipräsident into an ordinary president. Officially, the reason was that the original version might be taken to imply police approval of the printing firm in question.

Personal touchiness of public officials was everywhere a

Leopold Kraatz, Printers (The Chief of Police has no objection to *good* posters) c. 1912 (Germany) **Boda** (Above, before amendment; below, after)

Fin de Siècle (Illustrated Literary Journal) c. 1898 (France) *Alfred Choubrac*
(Above, before amendment ; right, after)

weak spot in the machinery of censorship. With advertisers and artists often ready to devote time—and even money—to making fools of them, censors were generally wary of compromise. The temptation to agree to the patching over of offensive matter was great—particularly where the alternative was complete withdrawal and reprinting. But on more than one occasion officials had been made to look foolish by agreeing to paste-overs. Patches often had the effect not only of drawing attention to the areas concealed but, if they bore wording, of producing hilarious side-effects.

The words *Appearing Next Week,* innocuous in themselves, could be disastrous when pasted across areas of the undraped female figure. Explicit references to censorship, sometimes guilelessly agreed to, were possibly worse. In one such case a poster showed a fully clothed female standing smoking a cigarette, with a dagger held in her hand at her side. The censor insisted that the dagger be removed. To avoid the cost of altering the poster, and to improve the shining hour, the advertiser submitted a sketch of the poster in modified form; a sticker had been pasted not only over the dagger but across the whole of the lower quarters of the figure. It bore the words *This portion of the poster has been prohibited.* The gambit failed. The censor disallowed it on the grounds that it would 'hold the censorship up to ridicule'. What's more, he added, it might come off in the wet.

(It was surely with suspicions of this kind, in the case of the Zaeo poster, that the National Vigilance Society declined the Aquarium's suggestion that the Society should paste over Zaeo's offending parts with 'printed matter of their own choosing'. Mr Coote was too wise a vigilante to be caught on that one.)

Of the cases where censors bloodied their noses on boomerangs, Choubrac's poster for the literary journal *Fin-de-Siècle* (pages 34, 35) is classic. Here, at some cost to both designer and advertiser, is the cover-up gambit at its most effective. If the original version was noticeable, the respectable version was more so. But this was no case for a genuine stuck-on patch; unlike the picture of the lady with the dagger, wet weather and inquisitive poster-peelers would reveal more than a dagger. Choubrac, the printers, and the proprietors of *Fin-de-Siècle* agreed to re-print the whole thing, this time leaving the censored areas as blank paper. 'This portion of the drawing' said the overprinted legend, 'has been prohibited.' Weather-proof and peel-proof, respectable yet titiliating—the decencies were preserved. Only in the vigour of the lettering of the prohibition do we see signs of shortness of temper. But he was not content to leave it at that. At his own expense Choubrac designed, printed and posted all over Paris a small final blow—a poster advertising scissors and fig-leaves. These, the devices of pictorial decency, the poster offered in a wide range of sizes, specifically for use on posters.

In Britain the tax idea gained ground. It would be so easy: Inland Revenue stamps would be fixed to each poster to a value commensurate with its area. It would bring in considerable revenue, would benefit those advertisers whose posters were overwhelmed by the mass of competition, and it would cut down the number of outrageous posters. It might even reduce the Income Tax by a penny or two. Said a London paper 'England is the only country in Europe which allows people to plaster what they like on vacant spaces in the public streets. Every Government on the Continent has widely made use of these street advertisements as a source of revenue, and of course,' (here was the darkest of all hints) 'the imposition of the tax carries with it opportunities for censorship.'

With a fearful eye over its shoulder at the Inland Revenue, the Censorship Committee of the Billposters pursued its work. That it did so in a mixed climate of public opinion, that it stood at the eye of the storm of prudes and permissives

Great Selection of Vine Leaves for Posters c. 1899 (France)
Alfred Choubrac

NOTICE

PROF. ALEXANDER

GENUINE HYPNOTIST, ELECTRICIAN AND BLOODLESS SURGEON.

Introducing MISS BERTHY BINGGALLI

The TRANCE MEDIUM, and the Famous ELECTROCUTION CHAIR, in which the Medium has passed through her body 150,000 Volts of Electricity without inflicting the Slightest injury. The Subject is also submitted for inspection to any member of the audience, and THE MOST MYSTERIOUS EFFECTS are produced by the Aid of Hypnotism, in which the Greatest Manifestations are obtained, the Clairvoyance and Somnambulism are remarkable and absolutely genuine and in this deep state of Hypnosis, Cures are Performed by me. Effects and Results of Hypnotism will always remain a profound Mystery, and in Genuine and Expert Hands good work is executed. Professor ALEXANDER is also at your service to TREAT CASES such as :—

SHELLSHOCK, PARALYSIS, SLEEP-WALKING, any Child who is Backward in Study, and BAD HABITS of any kind PERMANENTLY REMOVED, Etc.

Don't be afraid to offer yourself for Treatment, it will be FREE to you, and I also like to point out that I am not in discord with the Medical Gentlemen, as the Medical Profession cannot be done without, as there are certain cases which MUST require Medical Aid, and I can safely say that Doctors and Hypnotists of all Classes, Genuine, of course, always ought to work in Harmony and on friendly terms together,

Prof. ALEXANDER.

Moody Bros., Printers, Needless Alley, Birmingham.

alike, served only to sharpen the challenge. As a medium of communication, and as a bone of contention, posters were the big talking point of their age. Everybody had an opinion. Everybody expected the Billposters' Committee to listen to it.

The Committee relied strictly on its own judgement. Unencumbered with academic qualifications or high-flown theories, its members embodied a concept akin to that of the British jury. As they said in an early statement, 'Some of our critics allege as a bar to the right discharge of duties of censorship . . . the lack of proper talents, assuming that in order to duly discharge these duties the qualifications of a Royal Academician together with fine, exalted and superior sense are requisite. To this we answer that for the ordinary offices of life, that share of common sense which falls to the bulk of mankind, earnestly and thoughtfully used, is a better guide and preservative against error'. As men of the world, and above all as men of the poster world, whose knowledge of public reaction had become instinctive, they were especially well placed. 'The appointed Committee will have at least one important advantage, viz., they have been well drilled in the school of experience.'

Their experience was enlarged almost daily.

The committee had never regarded its machinery as infallible; clearly, there were many hundreds of posters too humdrum to receive submission; clearly also there were local and individual susceptibilities for which there could be no provision. For the large number of posters that never reached the hoardings at all the Committee was in no way responsible. These last were the remnant works of the fly-by-night brigade, the bills and small posters that were slapped up illegally on any vacant space. Posters of this kind, most of them concerned with cure-alls and Professor Alexanders of one sort or another, would automatically have fallen under the Committee's ban if they had sought admission to the hoardings. (This category was to remain active for more than half a century. The specimen illustrated is vintage 1916.)

Introducing Miss Berthy Binggalli 1916 (Britain) *Anonymous*

Even discounting the obvious hazards of non-submission and the outlaws, the variety and frequency of poster scandals was remarkable. With these, either formally or by invited comment, the Committee did its best. Sometimes its best was a word to the leader-writer of *The Bill Poster.* There was comment, for example, in the case of Mrs Ballin.

Mrs Ballin had written 'in the sacred name of motherhood' to the editor of the *Daily Chronicle* calling on county and borough councils and police authorities 'to veto improper posters'. These, she said, referring to some of the more lurid theatrical pictorial pieces, showed 'deformities and other objects calculated to injure the unborn'. *The Bill Poster* was deeply shocked. Reminding Mrs Ballin that 'in instructed opinion there is no probable connection whatever between such a shock as a pregnant women might experience at the sight of a placard and the birth of a distorted infant' it said that in any case there were no such bills. The Censorship Committee dealt with them relentlessly, long before local authorities or Police took it into their minds to interfere. And it saw fit to add how wounding and unjustified were attacks of this sort on innocent and unoffending people. To be held up to loathing as an enemy of future generations was by no means a joke. An apology was called for. 'Even a billposter,' said *The Bill Poster,* 'has his feelings . . .'

There was the case of the Improvement Department of the Cork Corporation and the Bovril bull. On Friday December 1 1894, Councillor Barry got up in the Council Chamber of the Municipal Buildings and referred to a matter which had been brought to his notice by the High Sheriff. It was a matter of certain posters in Western Road. It was a matter not only of their number but of their character. They were, he said, 'not at all suitable to the eye'. He asked that the Town Clerk be empowered to take them down and to see that no further such disfigurements, offensive to the eyes of young people passing by, be allowed.

On being asked to describe the placards, and their offence, Mr Barry replied 'I should be ashamed to tell you'.

As a sequel it was reported that the hoarding contractor had obliterated one or more copies of Bovril's poster painting by W. Watson RA, *A Highland Bull.* (There was to be a reminder of this story some fifty years later, when a news picture of a prize bull was obliterated, not as a whole, but, out of delicacy, in detail.) In the matter of the Bovril bull of Cork it must be recorded, to his great credit, that the leader-writer of *The Bill Poster* kept silent.

But if the Committee was to encounter offbeat objections, it was to have its fill of the ordinary ones. At its weekly meetings it lived on a steady diet of the staple ingredients—theatrical shock in all its forms, stranglings, shootings, hangings and whippings. But, predictably, it was nudity that caused the most trouble. As an item of poster stock-in-trade it was increasingly popular.

Inspired by the impunity with which fine artists exploited it, and leaning heavily on the justification of Art for the People's Sake, the advertiser sought not only to attract the eye but to confuse the issue.

Was not nudity the common currency of the galleries? Was it not universally accepted that the human figure was the most sublime expression of God's handiwork? Did not every classic artist paint from the nude? What about the many scores of examples of undraped statuary to be seen in our public monuments and architecture? Why pick on posters? All that the Advertiser was doing (he said) was to bring to the commercial scene—not before its time—the true touch of Culture. Those who objected to these things were either dirty-minded or ignorant—or both.

It was an argument that was difficult for the uninstructed to reject out of hand. Had not Michelangelo himself, and most of the rest of the great ones, reputedly painted little else than nudes? There was a serious risk of being taken for a philistine. It was difficult.

Le Journal ; Serial : The White Slave Traffic c. 1895 (France) *Théophile Steinlen*
(Left, before amendment ; above, after)

Difficult or not, after due deliberation the responsible citizen came down on the side of clothing. All over Europe the battle raged. One after another the bare bosoms of Lysoform ladies (page 17) were covered up. In Paris, no less a person than Steinlen (himself not far short of an old master) was obliged to comply (page 42). With the same dexterity that had marked their *décolletages* artists everywhere painted in compulsory *colletages*.

As usual, there were anomalies. Posters that were designed for international display fared badly. An acceptable un-coveredness in one country was often indecent exposure in another. The same poster could arouse admiration in Milan and a storm of indignation in Manchester. Exhibition posters suffered badly; with so many exhibitions based on themes that lent themselves to 'classic' poster treatment there was a glut of Greco-Roman pictorial statuary. Heroic figures—sometimes whole groups of them, all stripped for allegorical action —served as caryatids and banner-bearers. The arts and crafts, gas, electricity, industry at large, and almost every other aspect of human enterprise, were the subject of poster exposure. The International Exhibition at Rome in 1911 was typical. So was its reception. In the present illustration it appears with French titling, but there were some half dozen language versions, including English. It was accepted everywhere without comment—except by the Censorship Committee of the United Billposters Association. It did not appear on British hoardings.

Another design in similar vein, published in the same year to advertise the Turin International Exhibition of Industry and Labour, came near to the same fate. It also showed nudes (male this time) planting a flag-standard against a distant background of Turin. After due consideration it was passed by the Committee for display, but on the condition that it be 'posted as high up as possible, so as to be out of reach of possible mutilation'.

It must be said that the risk of mutilation was high; the work of dedicated addendarists was no less prominent in 1911

Rome International Exhibition 1911 (Italy) *A. Terzi*

ROME·1911 EXPOSITION
INTERNATIONALE

ART CONTEMPORAIN et RETROSPECTIF~MVSIQVE~ART DRAMATIQVE
ARCHEOLOGIE~ETHNOGRAPHIE ITALIENNE~CONGRES~SPORTS

than in later years. Their attentions led eventually to the establishing of an 'eight-foot limit', a height below which certain categories of poster were not to be displayed. The mutilation problem was universal; in Vienna a poster advertising the advantages of a public swimming bath was amended so promptly, so universally and so consistently that it had to be withdrawn immediately. The resource and inventiveness of the street free-lance has often taken the poster artist himself unawares; the Vienna case, featuring a drawing of two bathers, was described in a contemporary report as 'not without a certain imaginative flair'.

The mutilation factor was (and still is) undoubtedly a consideration, but there were (and still are) some who feel that it is either over-estimated—as in the case of the St Gotthard poster, which was banned because of the possibility of addenda—or used as a rational excuse when subjective argument fails. The St Gotthard poster was in all conscience an innocent enough production; the creative possibilities offered by the superimposed railway system must have been limited, to say the least. But it evidently caught the imagination of at least one censor. As a justification for suppression, the risk of mutilation is in many cases unanswerable, and it is accepted by advertisers only with reluctance. If objections are to be credible they are preferred to be intrinsic to the work itself, not to its potential as a point of departure.

Possible mutilation may also have been the cause of the rejection of Barribal's poster for *Who's Who?* Typical of a stream of such posters in the home-and-beauty years of World War 1, it was modified (page 48) to meet the requirements of civvy-street morality. But the addition of clothing also effectively protected it from risks of indignity.

The rehabilitation of wayward posters was a continuous (and, it must be conceded, monotonous) task. The published reports of the work of the Committee are intriguing, if laconic. The social historian must regret that many of the

St Gotthard Railway 1899 (Italy) *Anonymous*

Who's Who?

subjects of their comment have disappeared for ever. Here are items from agendas of 1904:

Pictorials: Letters were read from printing firms agreeing to accept the Committee's suggestions as to submitting sketches prior to printing bills of doubtful propriety. A letter was read from the Chief Constable at Oldham calling the attention of the Committee to the fact that the bill of a play entitled 'What a Woman Did', and which he described as highly suggestive of indecency, had been posted at the Colosseum in that town. This bill had been condemned by the Censorship Committee, and was consequently not posted by members of the Association, and the Chief Constable had been so informed. The Secretary was instructed to communicate with the manager of the Colosseum, the printer of the bill, and the owner of the play.

Our Christian Government and its Liquor Partners: This bill, representing dead bodies hanging by the neck from gibbets, was condemned.

The Convent Bell: It having been reported to the Committee that this bill representing a man in the act of strangling a woman with both hands round her neck, was being offered for posting, the Secretary was to apply to the printers for a copy of the bill.

What a Woman Did: An amended copy of this bill, in which, in accordance with the Committee's request, the bed in the picture had been painted out and the objectionable lettering removed, was passed as amended.

Queen of the Night: An amended copy of this bill, which had been altered by the obliteration of the red-hot end of a pair of tongs and the removal of objectionable lettering, was passed as amended, for the purpose of enabling the printers to use up old stock; but the Committee requested the printers not to reprint.

Women and Wine: An amended copy of this bill, which had

Who's Who? 1916 (Britain) *W. H. Barribal*
(See illustration page 24)

49

been altered by the removal of the knives in the hands of the two women and by the substitution of clubs, was considered. The Committee agreed that knives should be printed out, and a fresh copy, containing no weapons, should be re-submitted for consideration.

Transit of Venus: An amended copy of this bill, which had been altered by obscuring the right breast of the recumbent female, was passed as amended.

As was shown in the case of the Bovril bull, the imprimatur of the Committee was not necessarily a guarantee against let or hindrance. Of the poster for *Splash Me,* Southend's seaside revue, the local vicar said, 'I consider it indecent'. A London newspaper reporting the comment, expatiated on the evils of showbusiness as a whole: '. . . the suggestiveness of *Splash Me* is only equalled by the poster of the production, a poster which has caused the Vicar of Southend to make a strong protest to the management of the Hippodrome. The poster shows a girl in a pose which the Rev. Dormer Pierce is not alone in considering objectionable, and the bills of the production tell of beautiful bathing girls who do "towel trots" and allied suggestive gyrations.'

The vicar made his position quite clear: 'I do not think anyone can accuse me of being bigoted or a prude, but I have told the management of the Hippodrome that if the poster is not withdrawn I shall oppose the renewal of the licence. Of late there has been a tendency to go beyond the limit of decency . . . I have seen boys and girls attracted by this poster and giggling over its improprieties. A stand has to be made, unpopular though it may be, when things go beyond the limit.'

The London newspaper reported on the show itself. *Splash Me* is just what might be expected from the title and the poster. Its main object is to present a score or so of girls in bathing and swimming costumes, most of the costumes being just as

Splash Me 1913 (Britain) *James Affleck*

50

G. RAY PRESENTS A SEASIDE REVUE

SPLASH ME

abbreviated as any mixed audience would stand without protest. More than once these girls go through evolutions which can only be described as suggestive.' This seemed to clinch the matter.

The poster was covered. But the whole cast of *Splash Me,* reportedly incensed by the slur on its collective reputation, called at the vicarage to demand an apology. From newspaper reports it may be suspected that the visit was motivated more by an appetite for column-inches than by the demands of of honour. 'A red motor vehicle, chartered for the day . . . passed slowly through the High Street. The object being noised abroad, some two or three hundred people followed in its train. The inevitable snapshot man was present, and he had quite a busy time snapping pictures . . .'

They did not get their apology, and the poster stayed covered up. But thereafter business was very good. The Rev. Dormer Pierce was one among many who have found that in showbusiness nothing succeeds like denunciation.

James Affleck, designer of the poster and reaper of his own small harvest of publicity, declared himself 'quite at a loss to perceive wherein lies my offence'. With the full force of Michelangelo and the others to support him he reflected on the difference between the vision of the artist and that of the Rev. Dormer Pierce. 'The eye artistic sees that which is beautiful in nature,' he said, 'while, so it would appear, the ecclesiastical optic pictures only that which is vile; so piercing is the vision to discover indecency where none is intended that bath towels and even the ocean waves are as transparent as glass to its keen sight.'

So piercing was the vision in another case, Hjörtzberg's design for the Stockholm Olympics poster, that the banner-bearer was seen to be quite naked—which, like any respectable Greek athlete, he was. Here was another essay in classic nudity that came regionally unstuck; of the various language versions that appeared, the Dutch, the British and the Chinese required modification. There were observers who, when the modified version finally appeared, wondered

Olympic Games 1912 (Sweden) *Hjortzberg*

whether it might not have been better to have let it go as it was. The entanglement of the flying streamers, as well as being contrived, was odd.

Of the snares that await the poster designer, nudity is the most obvious. Less obvious is the Law's sensitivity about counterfeit.

When The Rank Organisation made a film of Mark Twain's story *The Million Pound Note* they took elaborate security precautions to see that the specially prepared note which appeared as star of the plot did not pass into general circulation. In spite of its improbable face value (and notwithstanding Mark Twain's point about the unpracticality of the high-denomination note) it was deemed advisable to keep a close eye on it. It was brought out of its safe only for as long as it took to get its image into the camera—and even then under guard.

The poster, however, was another matter. The design showed Gregory Peck chasing after the note as it fluttered away on the breeze. Only after the poster had gone up on sites all over London's Underground did the company bethink itself; might it be possible, if the original note was a matter for concern, that the reproductions of the note—crude as they were—were themselves a security risk?

The Bank of England was consulted. Yes, said the Bank of England, the reproductions on the Undergound were not just a security risk—they were illegal. They were a breach of Section 9 of the Forgery Act, 1913, and Section 38 of the Criminal Justice Act, 1925. It is illegal, the Bank pointed out, to reproduce bank notes *of any description.* The posters would have to be obliterated.

A squad of men went down into the Underground with black paste-over slips; they covered up the note. Later they went round again and covered up the whole thing with an alternative poster. Back at the Rank publicity HQ, remaining posters were destroyed. The million pound notes were gone forever.

The Million Pound Note 1954 (Britain) *Anonymous*

The Bank of England's veto was so effective that no copy of the poster survives. The illustration on page 54 has been taken not from the poster itself but from an adaptation that was used as an advertisement on the cover of a trade magazine a few days before the ban became operative. (It is reproduced on the assumption that the image of the note is here so indistinct as to exempt it from attention under any Act.)

It was the Law's intervention that accounted for the disappearance of the *Carry on, Cleo* poster. This too had had wide display on London's Underground before its enforced retreat. This too, for similar reasons, has become virtually extinct.

The film *Carry on, Cleo* was a parody of the film *Cleopatra.* The poster for *Carry on, Cleo* was a parody of the poster for *Cleopatra.* The Twentieth Century Fox Corporation, makers of *Cleopatra,* sought a motion in the High Court to restrain British film distributing companies from 'further reproducing or displaying any reproduction of a painting by Howard Terpning portraying Cleopatra lying on a divan, with Mark Antony and Julius Caesar in the background, or any substantial part thereof, in the form of posters, illustrations or advertisements without the licence of the plaintiffs'. They won their case. The court held, among other things, that because *Carry on, Cleo* was being generally released before the general release of *Cleopatra,* the impact of the publicity for *Cleopatra* was in danger of being ruined in advance. (*Cleopatra* had been running in London, prior to general release, for some eighteen months.) The offending poster was withdrawn.

Carry on, Cleo was not the only hazard that beset the Howard Terpning painting. As it originally appeared on tickets for the world premiere in New York the picture showed only Cleopatra and Mark Antony. Rex Harrison, who played the part of Julius Caesar, felt slighted at being left out. His portrait was added as a face peering through the curtains— 'a highly improbable grouping', as someone remarked at the High Court hearing.

(Above) Cleopatra c. 1963 (Britain) *Howard Terpning*

(Below) Carry on, Cleo c. 1963 (Britain) *Anonymous*

Following representations from the Twentieth Century Fox Corporation the poster for the film *Cleopatra*, which is referred to on page 56 of the text, and which it was hoped to reproduce here, has had to be withheld.

Henrion's powerful design for the Campaign for Nuclear Disarmament is one poster that did not appear on the Underground at all. Like many in similar vein, it fell foul of the *Conditions Covering the Acceptance of Advertisements* laid down by London Transport Advertising.

Under 15 separate headings, London Transport sets out the classes of poster advertising which it will not accept. These range through a predictable spectrum of sins: murder, horror, violence, indecency and obscenity; racial, national, political or religious controversy; extenuation of, or incitement to, the commission of crime; the fermenting of social unrest; offence of any kind, either through wording, design, or possible defacement; untruthful, 'knocking' or exaggerated statements—all are forbidden. So are unethical medical advertisements, direct or indirect references to contraception, and advertisements for films which have been refused permission for public exhibition.

This form of censorship (which is distinct from that operated by the Censorship Committee of the British Poster Advertising Association) is subject to no appeal and requires no statement of reason for its decisions.

Specific as the terms of exclusion are, it is to be noticed that, like the climate of public opinion at large, they are not without modification over the years. In 1964 article 3 of the Code listed the prohibition of advertisements that 'depict or refer to indecency, obscenity, nudity or strip-tease'. In 1967 the wording of this item was revised to read: '. . . depict or refer to indecency or obscenity'. There was silence on the subject of nudity and strip-tease. A similar change has overtaken article 11 which, in 1964, prohibited the advertising of contraceptives or direct or indirect references to birth control or family planning. In 1967 the prohibition concerning the advertising of contraceptives remained but the clause about references to birth control or family planning disappeared.

Like all forms of voluntary censorship, London Transport's

Campaign for Nuclear Disarmament 1963 (Britain) *F. H. K. Henrion*

code is a reflection of its own assessment of the temper of public opinion. Whatever its reasons for condemning the Henrion poster in 1959 it is not impossible that by 1979 London Transport will be judging posters of all kinds by completely different criteria.

With its apparently limitless capacity for intrusion, and with its knack of expressing itself with a maximum of impact, it is not surprising that the poster has sometimes itself suffered intrusion. The case is recorded of Charles Sayer Johnson, of Westminster, who in 1909 was arraigned at Westminster Police Court on a charge of wilfully and systematically damaging 'pictorial posters' valued at 3s. 6d. each. Caught in the act, he admitted with some pride that this was his fifty-first sortie. The posters in question were put out by a firm of brewers. They featured a dog looking at a glass of stout, under which were the words *What is it Master likes so much?* Johnson, a man described during the proceedings as 'of venerable appearance' and a man who felt strongly on the evils of alcoholic liquor, had added to each of these posters, in bright red paint, the words *The King's Doctor Says It's Poison.*

He said that he regarded the advertisement as a wicked question, but he promised not to do it again. He was ordered to pay one guinea costs. He indicated that his promise was not to be taken to mean that he would not chalk things on the pavement at the foot of the posters.

It was in the same courageous spirit, but conversely, that drinking drivers defaced the Royal Society for the Prevention of Accidents poster *One for the road may mean one for the grave.* This, one of a series of shock designs put out during the 'forties and 'fifties in the interests of road safety, was a much-defaced poster. More modest in size than Mr Johnson's subjects, and confined mainly to sites on municipal sand-bins, it was less conveniently placed for considered efforts, but whatever was going in the way of passing kicks, it got them.

Royal Society for The Prevention of Accidents 1953 (Britain) *Lynes*

ONE FOR THE ROAD

MAY BE
ONE FOR THE GRAVE

LYNES

**road safety
matters**

For the pre-breathalyser motorist, who knew that his driving improved with drink, the skull behind the beer-glass was a legitimate target.

In many areas of Britain, where local authorities were at liberty to use the poster or not as they wished, it was banned altogether. 'Simply horrible,' said one councillor. Plymouth Road Safety Committee gave a lead by announcing that, while it would stock the poster for supply to any organisation that asked for it, it would not display it itself. Many Committees that did accept it did so only after lengthy discussion. 'That,' declared a Bournemouth alderman, pointing to a copy of the poster as it hung on display in the committee room, 'that is probably a grave injustice'.

It is a matter for reflection that during this period, with accident figures mounting steadily, road-safety posters were probably the most banned. As in Victorian times, blood, death and destruction were greatly in demand for their entertainment value; when they were served up in relation to everyday reality, resistance was high.

Stable companions of *One for the Road* were a series of three, bearing the slogan *Road Safety MATTERS.* These (all of them formally banned by one area or another) showed respectively a woman collapsed over a telephone, a one-legged boy on crutches, and a little-girl road casualty held in the arms of a policeman. Like the skeleton motorist, all were the subject of harsh words, defacement, letters to the editor, and sometimes physical removal from their sandbins.

But most famous, most controversial, and most remembered of all British road-safety posters was William Little's *Keep Death off the Road.* This poster, published by the Ministry of Transport in 1946 as part of a major post-war campaign, caused a sensation that has still, some twenty years later, barely died down. It bids fair to take its place with *Bubbles* and *Your Country Needs YOU* as a poster classic.

Royal Society for The Prevention of Accidents 1955 (Britain) *Maurice Rickards*

63

The widow was a remarkable phenomenon. In a way that perhaps even her creator scarcely understood, she touched a deep and sensitive chord of response in everyone who saw her. The pallor of her face, the staring eyes and bloodless lips, the archaic widow's veil and the near-Victorian frame to the slogan—all these ingredients brought instant reaction, mostly of undisguised distaste.

She was not, as is widely understood, withdrawn as a result of the storm of protest and annoyance that she caused. She filled out her allotted thirteen weeks in the public eye (even overstaying a bit while the new Highway Code campaign was being got ready). What is significant about her, and what gives her a place in this collection, is that she is generally assumed to have been banned. It is perhaps symptomatic of the measure of the public's rejection of her that, whereas other posters disappear unnoticed from the hoardings, the Widow's departure was an event.

She was universally hated. Her very nickname, The Black Widow, sets the key. Her pallor, particularly, was hated. On scores of hoardings she bore signs of cosmetic attention—often carefully and sympathetically applied. Reddened lips and a rouging of the cheeks were unofficial contributions everywhere. Even the printers who printed her felt the need to give her a little colour. Mr Williams of St Michael's Press relates how he tried to sneak a little more pink into her cheeks. 'She looked unutterably miserable,' he writes. 'I couldn't help trying to liven her up a bit. But they wouldn't let me; they insisted on having that chalky whiteness.'

The image of her chalky whiteness was slow to fade. In a survey carried out some ten years after she had gone it was reported that people who had been children when she first appeared could still describe her in detail. Twenty years after she was still being referred to in the press as a familiar national figure (and still as having been 'withdrawn by authorities as a result of continued public outcry'). Of the many hundreds of thousands of copies of her that were

Ministry of Transport 1946 (Britain) *William Little*

**KEEP DEATH
OFF THE ROAD**

CARELESSNESS KILLS

Army Bureau of Current Affairs 1943 (Britain) *Abram Games*

Ministry of Health 194? (Britain) *Abram Games*

produced very few are left. She has become a collector's piece.

It might be thought that of the categories of poster least likely to be banned, those issued by government departments head the list. But this is by no means always true. Whereas in the case of the Widow banning was a fabrication, there have been notable cases where it was a fact. Among these (out of a total score of some hundreds of designs) Abram Games counts three casualties. One had to be changed, another was withdrawn, and another enjoyed only a brief existence before it was destroyed.

Best-known casualty was his ATS girl, a recruiting poster put out by the War Office in 1941. The design (page 71) was a success with the wartime public at large. It did much to dispel the image of the clod-hopping Army female—till that time the official archetype. It was welcomed by recruitment officers, who had called for 140,000 girls to fill the ranks. It also evoked criticism.

'Far too glamorous,' was the opinion in some quarters. 'We are not running a beauty chorus,' wrote someone to the *Daily Sketch*. Thelma Cazalet, MP, said it was 'not the kind of poster that would encourage mothers to send their girls into the Army'. She asked in the House of Commons for it to be withdrawn. Mr Bevin, Minister of Labour, reporting that opinion for and against it had been about equally divided, said that supplies of the poster were now exhausted and it would not be reprinted. The ATS girl was never seen again. She was replaced by a safer-looking version.

A design for the Army Bureau of Current Affairs, devised to convey an image of the bright new Britain, is the least-known of all Games' posters; this is the one that scarcely appeared at all. One of a series in which in a variety of fields, the New is seen to displace the Old, it showed a symbol of the bad old days—the figure of a child with ricketts. (It will be recalled that as well as slums, ricketts had been a not-uncommon feature of Britain's pre-war scene.)

'No,' said the proper authorities. 'Slums, yes—but not ricketts.' Admitting the existence of a serious disease of under-nourishment was more than even a Parliamentary democracy could do. The battle for the poster, with its shining symbol of Finsbury Health Centre and a clean new world, moved upwards. It passed through the higher levels of command till it reached the top.

'No,' said Churchill.

All copies of the poster were ordered to be destroyed forth-with. 'Very few managed to escape,' says Abram Games.

The small illustration, *Talk in here kills out there*, is a remnant in another sense. Even in this modified form, the poster aroused controversy. As part of a war-time security campaign, it was published to discourage hospital talk of troop movements and Naval and Air Force matters—facts and figures which might reach the ears of the enemy. 'The design,' said one newspaper, 'is the work of Captain A. Games . . . and is distributed by the Ministry of Health to meet an urgent security need . . . . It shows a man in bed, talking loudly enough for those in neighbouring beds to hear, while the Hun at the foot of the bed is smiling with satisfaction at reaping such easy "copy".'

According to the reports, men in hospital were tearing the poster down wherever they saw it. 'They object to the whole-sale display of this warning, in which they are depicted in their beds as screaming and gesticulating lunatics.'

One commentator described it as 'an insulting production, lacking in psychological insight'. Security Branch, who com-missioned the poster, were well satisfied. But the heat of the controversy over the poster as it appears in the illustration (and as it finally appeared on hospital walls) was as nothing compared with that produced by the version that preceded it.

It was a hospital matron who led the attack; she fought the poster on grounds both medical and ethical. Captain A. Games, of the War Office, Whitehall, had given his poster the

Ministry of Health 1962 (Britain) *Reginald Mount and Eileen Evans*

cigarettes cause lung cancer

caption: *Beware! There's a Jerry under the bed.* It was banned.

Nearly twenty years later it was another Government-sponsored poster, this time a design by Reginald Mount and Eileen Evans, that was to get itself censored. Again the Ministry of Health was to appear among the *dramatis personnae*. But this time the ban was imposed by none other than the Censorship Committee of the British Poster Advertising Association—descendants, in unbroken line of public conscience, of the original Committee of 1890.

Still going strong in 1962, their objection was distinct, immediate and unanimous. That cigarettes *may* cause lung cancer, said the Committee, is unarguable. But to claim, as the poster does, without reservation, that *Cigarettes cause lung cancer* is to misrepresent the state of medical knowledge. The addition of the words 'may' or 'can' before the word 'cause' would have rendered the poster perfectly acceptable.

The poster, like three others in the same series, was not modified by the Ministry of Health. Its display was confined to the non-commercial sites and sandbins made available by local authorities—and for which, said the Ministry, they were originally intended. The omission of the qualifying 'can' or 'may', it was explained, was in the interests of poster brevity.

The decision of the Committee, registered with the same finality as those of its forefathers, was entered in the appropriate space on the committee Report Form. It just said BANNED.

Ministry of Labour and National Service 1941 (Britain) *Abram Games*

A GAMES R.E.
JOIN THE
ATS
ASK FOR INFORMATION AT THE NEAREST EMPLOYMENT EXCHANGE OR AT ANY ARMY OR ATS RECRUITING CENTRE

Acknowledgements

Among the many organisations and individuals who have helped in the preparation of this book, the author and publisher would especially like to thank the British Poster Advertising Association for their kind cooperation.

Thanks are also due to the Staff of the Print Room of the Victoria and Albert Museum, to the Royal Society for the Prevention of Accidents, the Ministry of Transport, Mr Abram Games and Mr F. K. H. Henrion.